HOLLER AT YOUR GIRL

ASSAULT WITH A DEADLY WEAPON

EAST OAKLAND TIMES, LLC

EAST
OAKLAND

Do not let your hearts be troubled; trust in God.

JESUS OF NAZARETH

MY CRIME SERIES - BOOK TWO - HOLLER AT YOUR GIRL

Welcome to San Quentin State Prison! Come and meet your new "celly." Her name is Cjay and she has a story to tell about identity, loss, addiction, and self-love. Cjay has experienced great trauma in her life, however she has risen above the hurt and anguish. It is, though, a long road to redemption.

The books of the My Crime series are neither meant to justify nor condemn the inmates on whom they are written. Rather, the books of the My Crime series propose to candidly communicate the upbringing, life experience, and motivations of the incarcerated.

The My Crime series puts you as the judge. Your judgment will not simply be about the individual on whom a book is written, but your judgment will weigh the life circumstances that shaped his or her criminal disposition. The My Crime series takes the unknown inmate and presents his or her life for public evaluation.

Each book in the My Crime series is written on an inmate, by an inmate. Each book will progress from the Subject's childhood up through the commitment offense that brought about the Subject's current felony incarceration. Each book, therefore, will offer the big picture of the Subject's criminality as dictated to and written by a fellow inmate.

The My Crime series books are intended to fit into the present-day dialog on crime and punishment. As citizens of today's American democracy, the understanding we each have of right and wrong is the most essential knowledge we use in taking political positions. Ideally, the justice issued by legislators and interpreted by courts is a justice that agrees with most citizens. If citizens agree with the justice being issued by the government, citizens will promote that justice as truth for the times.

As a society, we do not know ourselves enough to have the right answers on justice. The My Crime series grants you the opportunity to sit and listen to the unknown felon and learn, as if you were on the bottom bunk, about your neighbor and what brought him or her to getting locked up.

Thank you for purchasing the second book in the My Crime series.

Encourage others to read the books in the My Crime series and please leave a review on Amazon.com.

I welcome you to visit the webpage dedicated to this series to access additional content for this book and other books in the My Crime series. **Additional content includes phone interviews, book drafts, and supplemental offerings:**

WWW.CRIMEBIOS.COM

Finally, I welcome you to read the last page of this book for information about the producer and publisher of the My Crime series, the East Oakland Times, LLC.

In liberty,

Tio MacDonald
Chief Editor

GIRLHOOD

My name is Cjay. I am a transgender woman of color, oppressed by the oppressor. I am on my 21st year of incarceration. My sentence fell under the California "Three Strikes" law. I received thirty-eight years to life for assault with a deadly weapon, a sentence longer than an actual murder. All the result of a "date" gone bad.

I was raised in Kern County, California. Kern County was growing at that time. More than anything Kern County was an agricultural area. There were many open fields to play in. We had a large backyard. There was also a swing in the front yard. I would reach such heights on that swing that I felt I would fly. Kern County was a safe but segregated. In whispers or in private we would call it "Klansville."

Despite being born male I was always a female in my mind. As a child I played with girls. I like playing athletic games, like Jax and Hop Scotch, or feminine games like dress-up. I felt the boys noticed me when we played dress up and I felt special. I felt like I deserved to be special for I was showing my truest self. It felt normal to me as I didn't like being a boy. I was never confused, I didn't like being male. I always knew who I was. Having a penis didn't make me male. Boys were rough and rugged. I was soft, sensual, and special.

My dad was a true alpha male. He stood at a full six feet seven inches tall and weighed 275 pounds. He was a heroic provider and very proud, especially of his children, his four boys. He scared me to death.

My mom was a soft-spoken and loving woman. She provided everything we needed and wanted. Our clothes were always cleaned and pressed. We had a hearty lunch to take to school every day. She was also an ear when we needed to talk to someone.

✗ ✗ ✗

One day my dad kept insisting that I go outside and play with the other boys. I told him, "Dad, I'm a girl." He dropped his cigar and turned around swiftly. This revelation did not sit well with my father. It was like I said a curse word. I was surprised he didn't kill me. I could see a vein on the side of his neck pulsate with every heartbeat. He looked for help from my mother, hoping she would say something. She stood up and exited the room.

My father and I argued most the night in an aggressive way. He kept telling me I was playing a game. I told him I was serious, that I was a girl. My mother did not intervene like I hoped she would. My brothers tried their best to avoid the conflict. They knew better than to challenge our dad. By the end of it, I simply let him vent. My mother eventually pulled him into the den and brought his favorite drink, Crown Royal on ice. After that night, he started tripping hard.

Life at home became a bit more stressful. I wonder if he thought he failed. He was the head of the Cary family, one of the most influential persons in town. His son could not want to be a girl. The barrage of words trying to change me never ended. Nearly every time I was noticed he would make a comment. He would talk about my mannerisms and my dress. He always referred to me as "son". In fact, he stopped calling me by my first name and strictly called me son. "Son come here." "Son do this...son, son, son." My father brought my brothers into the effort as well. He had me play the same sports my brothers played. I resisted more out of lack of interest.

Home became an awkward place to be. I was told that none of his sons would be gay. My father was stuck on making me a man. I told him I was not gay. I explained that I was a woman. Eventually I stopped talking to my father entirely. My brain was fried and my heart was broken. My mother became my rock even more as she spoke to me and loved me as I was. My mother was both encouraging and nurturing.

✖ ✖ ✖

My dad was a diesel truck driver. He started off small but was frugal and saved his money. My dad's hard work and my mother's business sense led to the company's success. We got to the point of having approximately twenty trucks, numerous trailers, a diesel lot, and shares in Chevron stock. Owning stock wasn't common in the black community at that time.

The business provided many opportunities for Kern County blacks and the community overall. My parents were likely royalty in town. Prominent persons, such as the mayor, would come by for dinner. Eventually, my brothers joined in the business and helped it grow even more.

My parents owned lots of cars. They were usually parked in front of our four-bedroom home. My father owned an antique Excalibur vehicle. That car was second to none in our area. It truly could only be outclassed by a Rolls Royce. He also had a Mercedes Benz. My mother chose to drive the Mark IV Lincoln Continental. When they drove together they would take the Cadillac El Dorado.

You can imagine some the bull that came with a prosperous life. Many people envied my parents because of the money and possessions. Everyone seemed to look at our family through a microscope, looking for the smallest misstep. Anything seen became town gossip. We became professional actors when we walked the streets.

Regardless of my father or the pressures of being a Cary, at that time my life was going pretty good. I had some really good friends. We mostly played neighborhood games. Many were sexual in nature. I noticed how the boys would want to play a game called, "Hide and Go Get It." In Hide and Go Get It you would hide and the person who was it would try to find you. Once they found you there was some sexy grabbing or wrestling before starting the next round. Another game was "Doctor and Nurse." The nurse always had the job of seducing the doctor. "House" was likely my favorite game. For House, there was a mommy and a daddy. I always played the mommy. In fact, I always played any role that put the boys on top of me. It was great fun and made me feel feminine. We didn't have intercourse but we certainly were grinding with our clothes on.

My brothers were masculine and would want to wrestle one another all the time. They enjoyed imitating what they had seen on television or they would put on eight-ounce boxing gloves and box the other boys in the neighborhood. My brothers never lost. At times, I would laugh as they knocked around the other kids from the neighborhood. My brothers also knew well the pressure from my father to be hyper-masculine.

As one should guess, boxing was not for me nor was it the type of physical contact I desired. I wanted to be held, kissed, and caressed. I did not want my lights punched out or to punch out anyone's lights. My game was flirting. I learned that attracting men was something I did well; it was my strong suit.

The struggle with my father never got better. Me being transgender and named after my father became unbearable for him. I was a son and that was how I was supposed to be. All the arguing and attempts to erase my identity culminated in me being sent out of state to be set straight. I was to be sent to Utah for military training, a type of boot camp.

2

SELF TRANS-FORMATION

What I found in instead, was myself at an isolated camp filled with lusty boys. I lasted only two weeks before being kicked out for sexual misdeeds. We got caught getting our grind on. My father was livid and told me not to come home. I was 16 and I didn't know what to do.

Near to the military academy was a town with a job corps. Somehow, I got sent there. I vividly remember driving into town. It was a picturesque type of place, quaint. The streets were lined with trees. Blue mailboxes were found on the corners. Couples were out walking and sitting on their porches. I thought it was great.

Job Corps was a program that taught employment skills. Primarily construction skills were taught. We stayed in single-sex dorms with approximately thirty people in each pod. The shower area was open stall showers where you could see it all. Little did my father know, I was in the best place possible.

At job corps, I began to meet other transgender people. I learned the basic "ins and outs" of being a woman. The guys would flirt with me daily. I learned to use what I had in absolute fashion. I was loving it and loving life. I was meeting people from all over the world and I had all sorts of companionships. I tried every nationality under the rainbow at least once. There were Mexicans, Jamaicans, whites, and blacks. You name him and he was on my plate. I was in heaven. Most of the men I dated were good lovers. I really don't have a preference.

Upon my return to California some years later I was different. I was 19 years old and I looked at sexuality different. I knew money could be made by having sex. A couple of people at job corps taught me that. California was slow compared to the lifestyle I now knew. I was bold and sure of myself.

At this point in my life I didn't care what my dad thought. I was living my life and I didn't need anyone's acceptance or approval. I worked for a short while for the County of Kern Bank. I was hired in a microfilm position for accounts receivable. With the money I made and saved from job corps and the bank, I was independent. I had my own place. It was a tiny one bedroom but it was mine. I also had a 1989 Honda Civic.

Nonetheless, I was not interested in the job. I dreaded waking up every morning to sit in a cubicle. I didn't take long to quit. Using my body could get me further and quicker than a 9 to 5 job ever could. I began a self-transformation toward prostituting.

3

MY MURDER THWARTED

With little time, prostitution brings in the quick buck. I was successfully making $1200 most nights. The downside to prostitution is that it is a dangerous game.

Once an average looking "Leave It to Beaver" white guy picked me up. He took me out to the desert. I thought, "This is a strange place for a date," but since he was paying I was game. We pulled off the main road and drove inland. There were no trees, nor vegetation. The night was shivering cold. The sky was pitch black. It was as if the desert was inhabited by evil spirits or ghosts. I didn't think about these things long. My thoughts were interrupted. He gave me three crisp one hundred dollar bills and we climbed into the back seat. The car was blue and had a blue interior with plush seats. It was an old car he told me he recently purchased at an auction. The car used to be a police car so the back doors only opened from the outside. He got out of the car and shut the door, locking me in the back seat. He went to the trunk and took out a gas container. I sat there staring. I had no thoughts. The moon roof on the car was open. He poured the gasoline inside the car and on me.

I was scared, frozen in fear, and gagging from inhaled gasoline. The gasoline smell nauseated me. I was confused. The man took lighter fluid from his pocket and squirt the fluid in my face. I was shivering and feeling numb. I pulled on the door lock to no avail. The door would not open. He took a small brown bag from his pocket, unfurling a packaged Bic lighter. I began to panic. I prayed for mercy. I needed a miracle. The man cursed me with the words "Burn bitch" as he wadded newspaper into a cone shape. He squirted the paper with lighter fluid. Now here is the miracle, which explains why I am alive to tell this story: when he flicked the lighter it burst into pieces. My heart slowed. I began to feel my fingers, as if the extreme cold had left. I could see his frustration. He was looking around for the lighter pieces. He mumbled something that I couldn't make out yet he couldn't put the lighter back together. I stared at the man and prayed and then everything went eerily silent. I blacked out.

The next thing I knew I woke up in the desert still locked in the back seat of the car. The man was gone. The sun was starting to rise. I could see animals running around. Every second it seemed to get ten degrees hotter. I was stuck in the desert in the back of a torture and murder machine. I tried to kick the windows out but they were reinforced. I tried climbing back into the front seats but the divider between the front and back seats was now locked. I searched around the car for water and food but found none. All I could do was hope and pray another miracle would come. I sat trapped in that car for three days.

I honestly give thanks to God for my survival. I saw a couple hiking through the area. I waved frantically for them. I was found by God's grace. They called for medical assistance and the search and rescue team came to my aid.

While sitting in the hospital I was questioned by the police about the events but I could not tell them I was prostituting so I turned silent. I gave them vague descriptions of the guy and the events and I was released from their interrogation. I was dehydrated and had not eaten or drunk anything all that time. A nurse provided an I.V. for my fluids. I had burns on my body from the gasoline. For the burns, I was given an antibiotic rub to apply on my skin. The nurse told me I was blessed to not have succumbed to the desert heat. I think it was God that saved me. There is no other explanation. The lighter was new. It should not have shattered. God saved me from a fiery death!

4

THE DOWNWARD SPIRAL

Now prostituting shined a whole new light on me, a dark light. My mind tripped and wouldn't allow me to fully do the job. I was afraid on the hustle. I was afraid of people and what people are capable of doing.

Being raped is common when you work the streets. You will always come across idiots that want to role play. Part of their sick fantasies are rape scenarios. They get turned on by it. I can't tell you on how many countless dates I experienced these violations. Here let it also be known, I consider it rape when you encounter a date that refuses to pay afterward!

At the time, my recreational drug use was what I considered normal. I wasn't addicted. I would smoke weed now and then and, of course, have drinks. Nothing heavy at that time in my life. Things changed when my brother Craig died. He was murdered in 1980. He was 17 years old. Craig is around one year younger than me. Craig was murdered in a drive-by shooting in Kern County. The police never found out who killed Craig or why he was killed. His death gravely impacted the whole family. It was the beginning of the end of my mother and father's 35-year marriage. They constantly fought over why he died. I don't know if my mom blamed my dad or vice versa. The issue was the razor blade that cut each of them to the bone. I tried to stay away. I had too much pain in my head and heart at that time.

As soon as I picked up the pieces from losing Craig, "Bam!" I was slapped again. In 1982, my second brother was killed. Kevin was killed in an Amtrak train accident in Tulare County. He was my rock and his death hit me like a sledgehammer. I could always count on Kevin. When Craig was killed two years earlier Kevin kept me from walking off the edge but now he was gone. I never felt so abandoned and alone in my life.

It was at that time that I went into a shell. I didn't understand anything. I was a walking zombie. The only thing that kept me going was strong mind-altering drugs. I began to use drugs heavily to take the edge off and calm my nerves. Try to understand that drug use in the 1980's was cool. It was like the 1960's hippie days all over again. It was what the cool and hip crowd did. It felt like there were never any overdose drug-related deaths at the time. That was until PCP came on the scene.

I used the drug PCP because it was the most effective. We called it by the street name, "sherm." It was the only drug strong enough to calm my nerves and all the B.S. going on in my head. I loved the drug because of its potency. PCP allowed me to forget the events happening in my life. It filtered all I couldn't filter naturally. It gave me a feeling of an out-of-body experience each time I used it. It provided a sense of strength, a false sense, to battle against the depression filling my heart. Soon it became a part of my every waking day. I was high on sherm all the time. The sudden deaths of my brothers were submerged by the drug. Their deaths took me down a deep and dark spiral.

PCP and prostitution went hand in hand. I was able to perform any task requested by dates. I needed sherm daily to block my conscience from evaluating the tricks I was performing. Sherm would blur faces so I wasn't sure what I was doing or who I was doing. Drugs over money became my main goal. Plus, I felt a comfort giving and serving. It gave me a sense, though a false sense, of being loved.

I did not have any PCP induced "rage trips" as seen in the media. Stories of people biting chunks off their own flesh or running around naked through the streets did not happen with me. I would smoke enough sherm to tranquilize an elephant. Even the good stuff that would leave people in zombie mode had a minor effect on me. People called zombie mode "getting stuck." What happens is a person's body freezes and won't move. I wanted to reach such a stage. I hoped to feel that way. However, I guess I was lucky to not have had such a trip. My highs were peace filled with a sense of joy and exhilaration. I wanted happiness and I believed that using was the key.

Drugs numbed my thought processes and my pain. I knew it wasn't good to use as I was. I did not believe it would be a permanent fix but it was there and I took it on completely. I was in self-destruct mode and had drugs on me 24/7 but not once was I caught.

My mother was also going through serious stages of grief. Her two boys, her wondrous and talented sons, left life before her and she was inconsolable. I listened to my mother and attempted to comfort her. She was grieving the loss of her two deceased sons who had passed within two years of each other: Craig my younger brother and Kevin my older brother, my rock.

Mom wouldn't stop crying. She would say to nobody, "I wish Craig was here to do this for me" or "If Kevin were here, that wouldn't have happened." The chores of life went on all around her but my mother no longer had the support she knew and in the place of the love and support known and felt, was deep grief and overwhelming loss.

I began to feel useless at home. My mother could not hear my words. She became unresponsive and mentally isolated. I was grieving as well. I also felt misery. Nevertheless, she was a wall, a wall that I could not climb nor push over. I knew my mother loved me and I am certain her intent was not to hurt me. She simply could not see me. I was there to love her but she saw right through me to her grief. Her grief was all she could see for it pooled in the tears of her eyes.

My mother never displayed any difference between the love she held for my brothers and me. From childhood, she had been my best friend; she showed love when my father showed anger and shame. She was always reassuring; she would say that everything would be okay. Now her reassurance and comfort were gone. Although she never said it, all I could think was that she needed a man's hand. She needed the comfort of a man and I, as a woman, was invisible to her.

Most transgender women I met did not know the feeling of being out in their femininity and being loved by family. More than often families tried to change us or threatened us to change. Please remember I am not talking about today's world of the openly transgender teen or child. I am talking about a time when transgender people and homosexuals were thought of as works of hell or mentally ill.

My brothers accepted me unconditionally. We used to talk about my gender. My brothers encouraged me to be who I was. They said that dad, in time, would understand. They helped me to feel loved and accepted. My mother did too. With their deaths, I lost all three.

5

L.A. LIFESTYLE

I needed a venue change so I got in my car and drove to Los Angeles. LA wasn't totally new to me as my father and I traveled through much of Southern Cali searching out different enterprises. I also had family in L.A. to help me get on my feet.

Looking for work in L.A. proved futile. I wasn't interested in most the available jobs so I had no money. Eventually, my unemployed status didn't sit well with my extended relatives. In fact, my younger cousins would cite me as an example of why they should get to loaf around. I knew I had to go.

The LA streets were much different and more dangerous than Kern County. From gang-bangers looking for a quick buck to psychopaths, it was important to know the ins and outs of the L.A. streets in order to avoid becoming a homicide. I took my time.

Women of all ages sell their bodies in Los Angeles. I met women in their 50's who said they had been ho'ing since age 16. Some of them took me under their wings and showed me how to operate. I learned where to go and where not to go. I learned the best places to take a date.

Not every woman is happy to see a transgender gal pop up on the scene. Of course, with all of us working it was also a matter of economics and I could certainly hold my own and then some on the prostitution hustle. I made money they could match but none tried to challenge me physically. They knew I would wreck their world.

Propositions for kinky acts increased ten-fold in L.A. Often the requests would blow my mind. Golden showers, fecal squats, S&M you name it. All these "johns" were ready to pay, but on some cases I drew the line; most I didn't. Being an awake and conscious hooker is not an easy job. You have to numb an inner voice to do it.

I started to build a client base. I got my grind on to the urban beat of West Hollywood and to the decadent disco of Beverly Hills. When things got slow I would send myself to Figueroa, the most well-known ho stroll in L.A.

Figueroa was a dangerous stroll that brought fast money. Sometimes the cash would come in so fast my head spun. Sometimes I found myself wanting to prostitute for the feeling it gave me. Other times, as earlier stated, I found myself weighing the money offered against a john's perverse request.

I was working seven nights a week and bringing in thousands of dollars, often in a single night. I spent my money as fast as it came in. I enjoyed luxurious sheets so I rarely got a motel. Hotels all the way. I enjoyed both the Hyatt Regency and the Waldorf Astoria. I always ate out for there was rarely time or mind to cook. You have to buy new outfits to wear also. I always bought top of the line clothes and heels. I needed the best make-up and lingerie. Plus, I needed to buy wigs. One will never understand how expensive wigs are until they become a frequent new purchase. Finally, I had to buy drugs and as my money went up so did my habit. I could spend great sums a day on getting high.

Another predominant character on the streets of L.A. was the pimp and every pimp wanted me in his "stable." A stable is the line of women a pimp has working. The pimp is supposed to protect and provide for his women. The flip side to the good is a dramatic bad, for pimps expect all money made from walking the streets to go to them. Therefore, it was protection at a price, a very high price. I didn't need protection as I could take care of my own business.

The pimps came after me like flies to doo-doo. In their close observations, they saw the money I was making and wanted it. I stayed independent. I was entreated by all, threatened by some, and nearly killed by another. The pimp who nearly killed me ambushed me with his goons. His goons never left his side so I could not win. On a later encounter, he pistol-whipped me. He hit me repeatedly across the face and in the stomach with his gun. I was kidnapped and kept in a garage for nearly a week. Every day he would talk to me about how he cared for me and all his women. He said he wanted me safe and he wanted to protect me. I had to work under him but as soon as my chance came I left. That happened during a prostitution sting. I left Figueroa with nothing but the clothes on my back. I couldn't imagine selling my ass and then giving the proceeds to an animal.

I left Figueroa and moved up towards La Sierra, another hoe

stroll. La Sierra was nothing like "the Fig" so I supplemented my income by stealing the belongings of dates. Some would pass out after sex. I would pack all their belongings in a pillow-case and leave them butt naked in the room. This was low of me but I knew they wouldn't call the police. In a short time, I recov-ered myself from the brutal losses of Figueroa. I knew how to get money.

Not too much time later I moved to an apartment in West Hollywood to live with other ladies who were also working the streets. There were five of us and we had an immaculate spot that cost a pretty penny but I was making more than enough. The single rule for the house was that no dates be brought there. We used the streets for dates and we vowed to keep our home safe.

The dates at that time in West Hollywood were brutal. The men were becoming evil and cheap. Some of the women couldn't keep up. Eventually, these women became a burden to my finances so I removed myself from communal living and freelanced at work and at finding places to stay.

By this time, I had become a veteran of the hoe hustle, the drug game, and the way of criminal enterprising. I found a comfort zone. People trusted me and confided in me. I was accepted by all the "throwaways" of this world.

I began to do something I hadn't done for some time: think! My parents raised me right and though we had our differences they loved me. I claim full responsibility for my own decisions and mistakes. I was acting a fool on my own accord. I was living contrary to how I was raised. I was doing what was contrary to my parent's wishes. I was in a daze. I thought solely in the present and in what I was experiencing at the moment. I hurt from my brothers' deaths and I struck out on my own. Now the care I knew growing up was shaping me into being a comfort for those truly at rock bottom, although I was at rock bottom with them.

By that time, I had been raped too many times to count. I never reported a single one. Mostly I just wanted to be paid but men often took me for their personal punching bag. I got used to it. Men would beat the hell out of me. I was used sexually in ways beyond speech almost every day. I was passed around and kicked out the door like garbage. Waking up to this took me time and age.

Drugs were still the major focus of my life. My drug focus did not change at the time; however, my drug of choice did. Sherm was a drug I would still use. Sometimes, I would use it to the point of no return, waking up unaware of my location, who I was with, or what I had been doing. Those times I often found myself robbed. Crack cocaine, "rock," was my new drug of choice. The more I used the more I needed. 100 plus dollars a day of crack rock found itself in my pipe.

I knew I had a monkey on my back. The drug game and working the streets became too much but also opened ways for me to meet new people, people who were looking to clean up their lives. Meeting such people offered a seed of hope for how I could be. Most people I met were ex-prostitutes. Most had the same experiences I had, of being used and abused by all around them. I was tired but I saw that transformation was possible.

For me, most of my criminal activities were based on the need to get high. Most of the work I did was under the influence of drugs. Drugs were the Dr. Jekyll and Mr. Hyde of my life.

Drugs settled down my nerves and made me feel at ease. Drugs provided comfort and even stability. However, as I needed drugs the drugs seem to need me so I had to get them and getting them brought me to the streets and to crime.

CALIFORNIA PRISONS

My prison career began with a four-year sentence. In 1987, I began serving time at California Men's Colony East (CMC) for burglary. I got caught with a man I thought loved me. He wanted a quick score because his money was low. We climbed in a house through a window and came out the front door with pillow cases of loot. Someone must have seen us for the front door is where we met the police. I was given a two-year sentence for which I served fourteen months.

I paroled in 1989. I started violating my parole right away. There weren't any new charges I simply kept violating parole. In the 1980's and 1990's prison was a place for transgender women of color to stay and be safe. We all stayed at designated prisons and we got along well. We learned to help one another. I was blessed to learn the true meaning of transgender sisterhood in prison.

Most of my time was served at California Men's Colony (CMC) and Vacaville. These two prison populations welcomed us. They were safe places to sleep at night. There wasn't much concern about rape so they offered a safe place to recover from whatever you were going through. We could get healthy from our time on the streets.

Employment for transgender women wasn't easy to get at that time. We were not treated with human regard. Most of us prostituted. We would take money or drugs from johns in return for sex. We put ourselves at risk of harm and incarceration. Usually, I was ready to go each time I was sent back to prison.

It is a sad but true fact that most of my medical attention was received at California corrections facilities. I had no medical insurance so in prison, I would receive the health benefits most people received with employment.

Prison also was a great opportunity to meet new people and catch up with old friends.

In the 1990's, conditions inside prison began to change. New sentencing guidelines and mandatory minimums brought about a rapid sentencing. Personnel transitions of guards and medical staff added to a changing climate in which transgender women became targets.

Guards often would let violators approach us or enter our cells. These encounters were ruthless. Violators often times would come up the losers, especially if they hadn't brought their goons to strike us down when we proved victorious. Violators would think twice about fighting me. I had been through a lot of dirt, plus I was born male. If a man lost a fight to a transgender woman, he never lived it down. His reputation was broken. Therefore, most men would only fight a transgender woman with a support-team in tow.

✖ ✖ ✖

One thing that never changed no matter what prison I was in was the men's need for sex. The men are horny and need sex. I chose to give it to them. I could have made good money if I wanted to but what I wanted was a feeling of love. I honestly did experience real love in a couple of relationships. Other relationships were for convenience or protection.

Some men in prison are the most low-down, wickedest people imaginable. For a period, I was being raped by a man and his crew. They raped me all night. Every one of them took his turn on me. I couldn't say a word to the prison guards for snitching is against the prison code. I became a victim and each night I was raped.

A sweet man in a nearby cell saw my predicament and faced the leader. He claimed me as his own. I am not sure how things were straightened out or if they had beef before I became involved, but he saved me.

I found true love with this gentleman. He helped clean me up and he made me his lady. After six months time, I realized that I loved him. He was the angel that rescued my wounded soul. We stayed as one for a time until I paroled.

From that point on I sought out good men, not abusers. I learned the difference between men's lust and men's love. Men in prison will lay up with you and make love all night. The sex can be magical and brutal at the same time. The next day, he will be up early and out at the visiting room talking with his wife and children. Men will do this in a blink of an eye. After getting roused up with his wife, he'll cut the visit short and be at your ass trying to get more. Most of the time I complied. Nowadays and for some time if a man has a wife and kids he is off limits for me. I am not a home-wrecker.

MY CRIME

Today I have been in prison for over twenty-two years. I am in prison for assault with a deadly weapon and because of the three-strikes law I have a sentence longer than a first-degree murderer. I will tell what happened.

I was in Kern County, Bakersfield. The day started off as usual with me on my hustle. It was daytime and slow and I was looking forward to evening. The freaks coming out at night is definitely true in the prostitution racket. There was a man sitting on a bench on our prostitution stroll so I knew he was looking for a date. I walked up and down the stroll shaking my ass but he simply sat there. I did not believe him to be a cop because there were no cars around for back up. I asked him for a light and I began to flirt with him. He was distracted from my words and gave the appearance of looking for someone. At that time I was using methamphetamines and my addiction was really gnawing at me. I needed to get high so I got a bit more aggressive with the guy. I figured he would like it once he tired. However, the conversation stayed aggressive and turned belligerent. He began to insult me and curse me out. I turned away and walked to my truck, holding an internal dialog as to my next move. The guy upset me so I decided to rob him. I grabbed my "Get Right" stick, a lead pipe, from my truck and moved on him for a jacking of his possessions. "Give me your wallet," I yelled. My goal was a quick come up without doing anything to him. As soon as I saw the whites of his eyes he took off running. I was wearing my full ensemble of high heels, dress, and wig so chasing him too long was not possible. I threw the pipe at him and, to my amazement, the pipe struck him on the side of the head. The man hit the ground fast allowing me to catch up to him. As he lay there bleeding, I rifled through his pockets. He had a wad of cash in his hand. I was scared to take it from him as he lay there helpless and bleeding. The incident happened swiftly. My heart was beating one thousand beats a second. My head was overloaded with thoughts. I actually robbed someone and hurt him without ever having that intention. I left the money in his hand and instead grabbed the pipe, not wanting to leave evidence. I ran back to my truck, a 1989 Dodge purchased by a date for me from the Dodge showroom floor in Bakersfield.

I started the truck and tried to drive calmly away. I took a few deep breaths as I drove to try and slow my heartbeat. It was a trick I used after taking a big hit of speed or crack. As I sat at a red light waiting for it to turn green my front windshield exploded. I was shocked into maximum alert. Then my driver side window exploded. Glass flew everywhere like raindrops. Next, I saw a ball of fire pass by my face. There were no other cars around, there was nobody visible until my ears alerted me from where the shots were being fired. Crouched beside a building was a Kern County police officer. He ran into the middle of the street and continued to shoot. My fight or flight impulse kicked in and I floored the truck's gas pedal.

In no time at all, I had three police cars behind me and a helicopter above me. I knew I would not get away but I also did not want to be shot. I began looking for a safe place to pull over. There was an intersection with a 7-Eleven. Students from California State University Bakersfield were all over the area, celebrating. I tried to make a sharp turn into the intersection but lost control. The steering wheel had a mind of its own and the brakes seemed to give out. The truck flipped over an eight-foot-high fence and dove head first down a river embankment. The truck ended up face down with the tail in the air. I could see water rushing nearby. I slid out the driver side door and ran toward a fence that enclosed the river. Running through the river seemed to be my only exit. The helicopter could be heard overhead and now I heard the sound of barking police dogs. I figured the man must have said I had a gun or that I had tried to kill him. I ran for the water. Officers stood watching on the other side of the gate. The water current was very strong. I removed the wig that I loved and cost me sixty-five dollars. Why I was thinking about a wig is beyond me. The dogs also watched me as they stood on the river's edge.

I exited the other side of the river. The journey was long and upon my arrival police cars pulled up with sirens and lights blazing. They screeched to a stop and rushed at me with guns drawn. In little time, I was on the ground with a knee in my back and punches and kicks decorating my body. I wasn't moving. I was in shock. They had the audacity to call me nigger. I really think if people weren't there it would have been worse. "We caught you black assed faggot," are the words by which I was lead to the squad car.

The police station brought on equally abusive treatment. I was handcuffed to the floor and abused.

To the man I harmed, I am eternally remorseful. He was a husband, father, son, and brother. I didn't know him, nor he me. My twisted way of thinking brought significant harm to his person and his relationships. For all of that I am truly sorry.

✖ ✖ ✖

One thing O.J.'s case taught most Americans is that freedom is possible if you have money. I had no money so I was issued a public defender from the state. For the preliminary hearing I entered a not guilty plea. Trial was set to begin in two-weeks. While in the holding tank, my preliminary public defender came to speak with me. He had barely touched my file as the papers he brought to review with me were unruffled and pristine.

His face was aghast as he read the police report. He told me, "Look we do not have a chance in hell to win this case. I suggest a plea bargain." I knew I was guilty of the crime so I was willing to plea to a lesser crime. Neither the judge nor the D.A. would hear that.

The trial started that day. I arrived in court at 8 a.m. We quickly picked the jury. The trial was over before lunch. The victim testified. The officers described my flight which brought about an accident causing the state damages. There were no more witnesses and both sides closed their case. The jury deliberated for a total of thirty minutes. I was found guilty beyond a reasonable doubt.

At my Romero hearings, an evaluation of my prior strikes, the judge declared that I was exactly the type of person for whom the Three-Strikes law applied. He felt I was remorseless and my explanations of the crime did not make sense. I was sentenced to thirty-eight years to life, twenty-five years for my third strike and thirteen years for enhancements.

When I reflect on the night of my crime I feel blessed to be alive. I truly believe if we had been in a location without other people, the police would have killed me.

SISTER TALK

Prison isn't designed to build you up, it is designed to tear you down. An inmate needs to believe in herself and learn to rebuild. Building yourself is the only way to make the time rehabilitative.

Here are the prisons in California where I have spent a large part of my life: I have been to Vacaville, a medical facility; I have served time at R.J. Donovan, located in San Diego; I have gone to Jamestown, which is better known as a fire camp; I was at the oldest California prison, Folsom State Prison; I was housed at Lancaster (California State Prison) when it was black operated (most prisons are staffed by whites or Hispanics); I also stayed at the deadly level 4 prison in Tehachapi; today I am housed at San Quentin.

Through the Restorative Justice curriculum offered at San Quentin I now more fully understand the harm brought about by my ways. I understand and feel a responsibility to the victim, his family, and the community I lived in. I have shame and embarrassment for what I did and I will make amends in whatever way I can.

I have missed out on much of life, life's simple treasures. I missed the family gatherings, graduations, marriages, births, and sadly, funerals. I missed the funeral of my niece who passed young. I missed the funerals of both my parents and my grandmother. Each of these three persons raised me, suffered for me and beside me. I will always love and miss them. Being absent from them in their final days is something I have a hard time forgiving. Guilt will forever be a lamented but integral part of my soul. I do not believe it will leave me for they deserved better. I should have been there to ensure they were laid to rest with dignity. They loved me in life, I simply hope they can forgive me in death. I was truly out of control.

I have twenty-two years in prison and I'm fifty-eight years old. My body feels the aches and pains. I never thought getting older could be this difficult. Freedom, however, isn't all about physical movement. Personal growth can make one free. Living in God's grace can make one free. I have wanted to be a better person and that began with me forgiving myself and facing my own personal demons. I am a transgender woman of color. I am not a criminal. As I look back over my years of life I consider my need to feel accepted. I sought acceptance or value through drugs, through crime, and through sex. I no longer need anything exterior than God's love. God's love sustains me.

I live recovery every day. The things or stimulus I thought to be important in my younger years now have little meaning for me. Prison has more downs than ups but although I am in prison, I feel free. I have a sense of purpose in life. I have faced the sexual abuse, physical abuse, and drug abuse I knew in times past. I have learned to accept myself and forgive myself for my mistakes. I have also learned to forgive those that harmed me and to seek forgiveness from those I have harmed. I am deserving of real love. God loves me, this I know, as much as He loves anyone else on this planet. I am worth it.

I am serving thirty-eight years to life sentence. Without the three strikes law, my case would have carried a seven-year maximum. My sentence will not destroy me! I think about the harm I did and did not get caught for and I weigh it all on a cosmic scale of justice. I feel no bitterness. The pains of age and the pain of being told day in and day out what to do aren't becoming easier but looking myself in the mirror has become a gift to me from on high.

Today I want all my sisters to know that you are beautiful and unique. You are one of a kind, created from God's grace and love. God makes no mistakes. Be good to yourself. Through pain and fire get yourself together now!   Tune into your spirit and get your hands dirty, rid yourself of junk. Shake out any mental handicaps a lover, boyfriend, or whoever has put on you. Accepting yourself will change your thinking. Go to self-help groups! Align yourself with what is offered by the community. Get yourself together and then you will find new possibilities. You will find someone that is going to love you the way you need to be loved. You got to do the work in order to receive the love and life you deserve. Love yourself! Love life! And remember to "Holler at your girl!"

FORWARD TO FROM HOOD TO HEELS

Lawrence was sentenced to life in prison. He owned and drove the car sighted in a gang-related killing. As a leader in a bloody feud with a rival gang, Lawrence had, for some time, terrorized Los Angeles' neighborhoods. Before his arrest, he sensed his days on the streets were numbered. As a financial precaution for his absence, Lawrence purchased sums of larger sized clothes for his infant son.

Lawrence's intuition was correct, he was to leave the streets, yet Lawrence could not have mentally conceived the true transition that lay ahead. Lawrence was on his way to becoming Lauren, a transgender woman of color.

"From Hood to Heels" is the unbelievable true story of a child raised in violent circumstances who became the epitome of extreme violence while at the same time holding tight to an inner secret of female identity.

"From Hood to Heels" presents two stories in one: first, the personal experience of a child born in violent circumstances; you will come to know the world of drug dealing, gangs, and violence. You will grow uncomfortable as children make life and death decisions that often increase the circle of violence. You will find out how crimes, such as carjackings and crack dealing, are perpetrated. You will witness the racial divisions found in Los Angeles neighborhoods pitting Hispanic gangs against black American gangs. The first story of 'From Hood to Heels' is a true American tale of a life born behind the 8-ball as told with gravity, frankness, and doses of humor.

The second story marks the birth of Lauren, a transgender woman of color. The second story reveals the deliberation period for a person in identity conflict. You will stay up late with Lauren, as her mind swirls in the consideration of who she is. You will cross bed bunks with Lauren as she carves out her sexual identity. With Lauren, you will visit the prison psychologist and with Lauren, you will confront former gang associates as they challenge Lauren's identity change.

"From Hood to Heels" is the story of Lauren, her upbringing, her adolescence, her crime, and her transition into womanhood as told by Lauren to a fellow inmate writer.

The East Oakland Times, LLC welcomes you to purchase the book today. "From Hood to Heels" can be found on Amazon, Audible, and at www.crimebios.com

✖ ✖ ✖

From Hood to Heels

East Coast Crips was my life. I lived for my hood. I gave it my all. I was completely loyal to it. I didn't realize it until I was fighting this case, that I had already built a major reputation. I was still going hard when all I had to do was just kick back. When my name came up, it held its own weight. I rank my gangsterism at an eight and my gang, East Coast Crips, a most definite ten.

Yet, in spite of this, here I sit. I'm in prison for a gang murder. I was locked up when I found out that Charlette was pregnant with my daughter, Ahniya. The sad thing is, I have never been home for my baby girl, and I only got to be with my son for nine months.

I thank God every day for Charlette because she was strong enough to stand by me and she keeps the kids in my life. Even though from behind bars I watch them grow up, I am counted amongst the blessed. In 2015, Charlette agreed to marry me and become my wife. Together, we work hard to keep our family together and my kids going down the right path.

✖ ✖ ✖

One of the bitterest pills I've ever had to swallow, was being locked up when my mother passed away. She died from kidney failure just like my grandmother, Queenie, did. At the time, I felt as if I wanted to die also, but my children kept me strong. I was twenty-five years old.

My mother's death caused me to run head first into a wall of reality. I was wilding out and getting into all sort of trouble in here, but when she died it caused a fundamental shift in me. I grew up.

One memory I hold as sacred as a religious person does her deity. See, I never finished high school, but in prison I obtained my GED. Getting my GED felt as if I was working a job all over again but it felt great accomplishing something. Even though I was confined when I obtained my GED, imprisonment in no way diminished the joy.

My mother was alive and got to see me achieve this. Just hearing her voice telling me how proud of me she was, made me just as proud as I was on the day my son was born.

✖ ✖ ✖

The proudest moment in my life however, came on the day that I stopped worrying or caring about what other people thought about me. It happened in 2016. That was the day I allowed Lauren to be born. I say this because I stopped hiding who I truly am: I am transgender.

Obviously, by my story, one can see that I have not lived my life as a transgender on the streets, but I have known since the age of ten that I was different, born in the wrong body. I hid who I was. I let the pressure of what others, mainly my father, would think of me keep me from being myself. Even though I had these feelings, I didn't want to disappoint my father, or even worse lose his love for me. As I mentioned before, my father was a strong male figure in my life. He was one of those macho men who thought everything was a test of manhood.

I was ten when we had an incident at home, when some female panties popped up in our laundry. My father went crazy, questioning my brother and I about who they belonged to. He was furious and asked if one of us was "gay."

I will never forget the angry look that filled his eyes. But, that still wasn't what caused me to hide myself and my emotions.

My brother lied and told my dad that he'd had a girl over and she must have left the panties. The look of relief that came over my dad's face was unmistakable. The words he uttered are what kept me hiding myself for twenty years. He said that he was sorry for accusing us and that his biggest fear in life was that one of his sons would end up being gay. His words became inscribed cornerstones of my fear. They rang in my mind for years. I could never tell him that I had actually stolen the panties from one of his girlfriends.

Even still, not even my father's persona stopped me from feeling like I should have been born female.

I did everything my dad wanted. I played sports and lifted weights. I dated girls and even lied to my father about me having multiple girlfriends, just so he would be proud of me. I lusted after women, but in truth, I was actually envious of them. I couldn't shake my father's words so I went on to have two beautiful children. Now make no mistake, I have no regrets about my children being born. However, I do wish I could have been strong and been the person I felt I have always been. Maybe I would have saved myself a lot of pain and grief. I probably wouldn't even be in jail now. It's a hard thing to not care what others think of you. Eventually, I had a breaking point when I was unhappy because I was faking about who I truly am.

All my life while committing crimes and gang banging, I still knew that I was Lauren but I became extremely skilled at hiding things. For example, I would be chilling with the homies in the hood and underneath my clothes, I would be wearing some panties. I even went on a few missions wearing thong panties. Never once did I give consideration that if I got caught and went to jail, my secret would be revealed. Hell, I'd even dress up in women's clothes while locked in my room.

For a long time, while incarcerated, I hung around the transgenders. Everybody thought I wanted to get with one, when in truth, I wanted to be one. I had a friend who was feeling like me and he found the courage to begin his transformation into she. I thought that I could never make such a move because I was now married, plus, a lot of people knew me and looked up to me as that vicious gang banger, Pitch Blacc. Inside, I was hurting beyond measure, so much so that I decided to speak with a psychologist about how I felt and how exhausted I was with hiding myself.

I was eventually diagnosed with gender dysphoria and placed on hormones. I didn't realize how easy and fast things would change for me. My entire life, I acted like a man, yet soon after taking hormones, people began noticing the changes and would tell me that they couldn't picture me acting like a guy. My facial features softened and my breasts grew. People began treating me like the woman I am.

Everyone transitioning woman has her own story about the things she has been through, but so far, I'm happy to say, in my transition, I have not experienced too much negativity. I built a reputation for myself and I believe that, along with the fact that I am in here for murder, has played a major factor in why. I am treated with respect, and being Pitch Blacc has helped a lot. Plus, I treat everyone with respect. I have always been told that I carry myself with respect. I don't try to fit in with people, I just do me.

I still go to the basketball court and play ball with the guys. Of course, there are times when I get those weird looks and even a few laughs. That lasts until the ball is in my hands and I cross a guy over. Then, everyone looks at me as a girl who can hoop.

So far, all of my gang member family I've run into still show me love and respect. I've even been flirted with by some of my homies. I have had only one negative incident with a gang-banger. He was my homie named Bam. He was from my old hood. He had a problem with me changing.

Now, even though I have changed physically and somewhat mentally, I still have that thug mentality. I don't allow anyone to get over on me. There was talk on the yard that Bam had said some foul words about me now being Lauren.

Other homies that know how I am, quickly sent word to Bam letting him know that I was looking for him so that we could address the issue. He sent me a kite (note) explaining himself and telling me that he didn't mean any disrespect. He went on to state that it was hard for him to understand my sudden change.

He reminded me that we were comrades from the streets and that we didn't see this kind of change in our hood. He ended by saying that he felt as if he had lost a soldier, but that if I was happy then he was happy for me.

When we were face to face, I let him know that he didn't lose a soldier, and that I was still me. All the thugging we'd done, was still inside me. He gave me a hug and we are on good terms.

Recently, during a visit with my dad, my wife, and my kids, I revealed how I now look to them. Now, they had spoken to me on the phone about my transition, but they were shocked when they saw me. All of them said that I look like my mom.

I know that I am lucky because everyone has accepted me for who I am, especially my dad. He told me he didn't remember all the things he'd said to me all those years ago, and that he was sorry that he had. He said that he wished I would have told him how I felt a long time ago.

I know that if I had been Lauren on the streets, I would have hung around a different crowd. I would have had different friends. I am just glad I found myself now, because I know some people never truly find themselves.

I do regret that my mom never got the chance to meet her other daughter, me. I know she would still have loved me just the same.

Honestly, I have to say, I blame no one for my involvement in crime. I am a smart individual, raised to do the right thing, but I chose to do wrong. I couldn't wait and work for the things I wanted, like most people do. I fell for what the streets showed me.

Yes, I worked and respected the decency of honest money, and even felt good earning it, yet something inside of me made me lust for more. To satisfy that lust, I did bad things to get what I wanted faster.

Even still, I know the things I have gone through have made me who I am today. It is all for the good because at one time, I was truly becoming a wicked-hearted person. I was surviving and I refused to be looked at as weak or a victim. Yes, I wish I could have accomplished more positive things on the streets, but I can say that I know my own self-worth now. I know I am capable of great things. If I could change my life path, I would most definitely remove from my history getting a life sentence, yet I know how I lived. Still, I do fully regret cheating myself of the opportunity to be in my children's lives. Even so, I cannot stop writing my own story.

EAST OAKLAND TIMES, LLC

The East Oakland Times, LLC (EOT) is a multi-media publication based in the San Francisco Bay Area. Founded by chief editor, Tio MacDonald, EOT has at its core two principles: the principle of the dignity of life and the principle of liberty. EOT supports the flourishing of humanity through peace. Peace will be found when persons honor the principle of life's dignity and the principle of liberty.

Current Projects Include:

- Publishing of the My Crime Series
- The Publication of Original Inmate Art and Books
- Podcasts from California's Condemned Row
- Quarterly Print Publication for Free Distribution on the Streets of East Oakland
- Website Dedicated to Inmate Reporting on Current Events

Please remember by leaving a review you encourage others to buy the books in the My Crime series and thereby YOU support EOT's mission. Please leave a review at Amazon.com.

For exciting My Crime series bonus materials, such as original documents used for the composition of the book, go to www.crimebios.com

Support the EOT by purchasing EOT produced e-books, print

books, and audiobooks!

Be positive!
Be and stay blessed!
Do good!

Tio MacDonald
East Oakland Times
Chief Editor

EAST OAKLAND